It Was Not My Time

Anna Mitchell

RIVER BIRCH PRESS

Daphne, Alabama

It Was Not My Time
by Anna Mitchell
Copyright ©2020 Anna Mitchell

Unless otherwise identified, Scripture is taken from *THE HOLY BIBLE: New International Version* ©1978 by the New York International Bible Society, used by permission of Zondervan Bible Publishers.

ISBN 978-1-951561-44-4 (Print)
ISBN 978-1-951561-45-1 (E-book)

For Worldwide Distribution
Printed in the U.S.A.
River Birch Press
P.O. Box 868
Daphne, AL 36526

To Mike, Jordan, and Ian
You are my reason
My love for you is endless

Contents

Introduction

As a stage three breast cancer survivor, I'm a living testimony that God still performs miracles today! As you read this book, you will be taken on a journey of insurmountable strength, unwavering faith, and unbreakable trust. Although I've been blessed with a strong will and positive outlook, it is the power of prayer and my deep faith in God that ultimately led to the absolute greatest day of my life—my physical healing on December 17, 2017.

As of today, one in eight women will be diagnosed with breast cancer. Isn't that an unfathomable and sobering thought? This book tells the story of how God chose me to experience what so many others are going through or will go through. My journey is one of joy, and although I wouldn't have chosen this journey, it was chosen for me.

Earlier that year I did my annual mammogram and just like every other year, the results were negative. Only a few months later, I found out I had stage three breast cancer. I felt devastated and didn't know which way to turn. I searched for a quick fix, but it didn't take me long to realize that God was the answer.

During the initial shock of my life, I had to make so many decisions while my mind was ping-ponging between stress and anxiety. My life was hanging in the balance. Sure, I'm strong, but this needed more than me. This needed the One who created me, and we were going to fight this together.

The faith I thought I had was nowhere close to the faith I developed. It is so true that you don't know how much you need Him until He's all you need.

As I share my story with others, I sometimes feel I'm

being judged, and many times I get questioned, "Why you?" Some people want to know why God healed me and not someone they knew who died. I always give the same answer and that is, "I don't know, but what I do know is that He knows." He knew it all before I did. I'm sure I will be asked this question for the rest of my life, and I will keep giving the same answer. He chose me and wants me to let the world know that He is real and He heals.

After my healing, it took months to realize that I have the answer to why He healed me, and it's very simple. I have learned not only that He loves me, but He is indeed faithful. He answers prayer. He answered mine. He has always been close to me even when He felt miles away. He fights my battles with me and for me. Everything always works out the way it's supposed to. If it doesn't go the way I prayed, I know that was His will, not mine. He waited patiently during my entire life for me to finally put *all* of my life into His hands and to completely trust Him. He kept His promises, and I know He always will. I am forever grateful and honored that He chose to heal me.

ONE

Everyone Has a Story

Just like every other year, I had my mammogram and well-woman checkup at the beginning of 2017. A couple of weeks later, I received a letter in the mail with my results, saying that my mammogram was normal. I thanked God and threw the letter in the trash, which had been my routine year after year.

About two months later, when I was getting ready to go to work and putting on my deodorant, I felt a quick, sharp pain under my right armpit. I didn't think much about it because I had felt this a few times in the past. I tend to diagnose myself because I feel that I know my body pretty well. I'm not sure why I do this. Maybe it's because I have such a high pain tolerance, or maybe it's because I've never had any serious health problems. Two more weeks went by, and I still felt the same pain. I thought it seemed to last a little longer than normal, but I figured it was benign cysts, and they would go away as they always did. I kept thinking I was okay because my mammogram results said I was.

One day, my right breast felt swollen. I thought to myself

that it was weird and maybe something was wrong. Again, my mind referred back to my mammogram results. It never crossed my mind that I could have anything too serious, especially cancer.

When I got home from work, I gave myself a breast exam. I felt an awkward shaped lump, but it was soft. Like many common myths about breast cancer, I had heard that cancer feels hard as a rock, like cement. It didn't feel like that, so again I wasn't too worried. I actually felt a sense of relief that my lump wasn't hard, but I kept wondering what in the world it could possibly be.

I already had a doctor's appointment scheduled with my ob-gyn for some menstrual complications I was having before any of my breast symptoms appeared. When I saw my doctor, I mentioned the lump in my breast. She examined me and said exactly what I had been thinking. She said "That is weird. If it gets worse, come back for an ultrasound." I said okay, got dressed, and went home.

About a week after that appointment, I started to feel a burning sensation, so I called my ob-gyn back and made an appointment for the ultrasound. A couple of days later, my burning seemed to be subsiding so I was going to cancel my appointment. My sister and I are extremely close and share most everything with each other, so I called her and explained how I was feeling and that I was going to cancel my appointment. Why keep my appointment when I was feeling an improvement? She advised me to go to my appointment so I would have peace of mind, but I kept debating. I struggled for a couple of days because I was just too busy between work and life in general to interrupt it with another appointment.

Then a day or so later, I saw redness near my nipple. I was confused at this point. I was thinking that something must be wrong and that was enough confirmation for me to keep my doctor's appointment. Again, I didn't think the symptoms I was experiencing would ever be breast cancer, especially that awkward lump that didn't feel hard. Thank God my sister convinced me to keep my appointment because it could have very well saved my life.

In May, I woke up and got my son ready for his day and drove him to school. I went home to get ready for my doctor's appointment and drove to my ultrasound. After my appointment, I was planning on going straight to work. I was completely worry free. I just wanted to get the appointment over so I could get to work as soon as possible.

There had been a few days at work when I had felt more lethargic than normal, but I always felt a little tired because I toss and turn a lot throughout the night. A couple of those days I felt as though I couldn't get up from my chair. I almost felt paralyzed because my body wouldn't move. Even getting up out of the chair all of a sudden took so much energy. Why was I feeling this way? This was not a normal tired. There were so many signs that I had breast cancer, but I didn't listen to them because I believed the myths and trusted my mammogram results.

As I was laying on the exam table, I started to wonder what the technician was seeing. Cancer still didn't cross my mind. Once the ultrasound was over, I got dressed and started to say goodbye. The technician stopped me from leaving and said she needed to show the ultrasound to the doctor and asked me to sit in the hallway.

I had ultrasounds in the past, but I felt something must be

wrong because usually the technician walks out of the room to have the doctor look at the ultrasound during the procedure, not after. The technician came back and said to continue to wait where I was sitting, and the doctor would be with me shortly.

I couldn't believe it, I knew right then and there that I had breast cancer. My mind instantly began spinning. It was going a thousand miles a minute. I started to panic, and almost began to cry, but I told myself to stop because I wasn't one hundred percent sure. I waited about twenty minutes, which felt like the longest twenty minutes of my life. Finally, the nurse came and got me and walked me to the exam room. I'm pretty sure that was the longest walk down the shortest hallway I had ever made.

I walked into the room and sat in a chair where my doctor confirmed my thoughts and told me that I indeed had breast cancer, and that I had multiple tumors. It took every bit of my strength not to start bawling; my mind began to spin again in a million different directions. I've never experienced so many different emotions all at once, and there was no one with me to share what I was feeling. I asked her the first thing that came to mind, "Is it in my lymph nodes?" and she said yes. I felt my body slump and my heart sank. Again, another myth that I had heard was that when cancer spreads to the lymph nodes, you die.

I looked at her, rolled my eyes, and said, "Oh my God, I'm going to die!"

She replied, "Oh no, breast cancer treatment has come a long way and hardly anyone dies from it anymore."

So I clung to those words, accepted them, and went numb. I had tears in my eyes, but I didn't cry. She asked me if I heard and understood what she said because I guess I was acting as if I hadn't. I replied that I heard her and understood. I was devastated, and it felt as if life instantly stopped and nothing mattered, nothing! My mind wouldn't stop twisting and turning.

My doctor didn't want me to leave without having a set appointment to see an oncologist, so back to the hallway I went, and sat there by myself after hearing the worst news of my life. While waiting for the receptionist to make the oncologist appointment, I still felt numb. The receptionist told me that the oncologist wanted me to bring a record of my mammograms with me to the appointment. I was dazed and not ready to deal with it, but I didn't have a choice. I couldn't call to request a copy to be mailed to me because my appointment was only a couple of days later. Even though I had a couple of days to get my results, I felt I needed to get them right away. Before I drove home, I went to the medical center to get the mammography records. When I got there, I could barely keep myself together because I wanted to scream at them for not catching my cancer. I was very upset and disgusted at the same time. That was a very difficult moment.

When I got back into my car, I finally allowed myself to cry for a few minutes, but I needed to get myself together to drive home. On the way home, I called my husband and told him the awful news. I felt bad telling him over the phone, but I couldn't wait any longer and he needed to know. When I got home, I called my boss and told her I needed a few days to get my thoughts together, and she completely understood. Actually, I never got myself together enough to go back to work.

The thought of telling my boys made me cry hysterically

as I knew it would change them forever. That night I told them separately. I could see in their faces that their hearts were heavy, and I knew their minds were spinning as well. I shocked them with quite possibly the worst news of their lives, and I'm sure they were thinking that their mom might die. They were both speechless. I will never truly know what those words did to them. All I could do was pray. They were going to watch their mom fight for her life. Nobody deserves to watch their mom fight for her life.

My oldest son talked to me about holistic medicine. He felt that chemotherapy would kill me or damage my body so he wanted me to try what he thought was the best treatment for me. I disagreed and told him that I felt my cancer was too aggressive for holistic treatment. I don't have anything against holistic medicine, but I chose to fight my battle with chemotherapy. Although not knowing the end result, I assured them that I was going to be fine. I fought and stayed insanely strong for them because I love them so much. My boys are my every breath, and there was no way I would let breast cancer take me from them.

It was two days from the time I received the news from my ob-gyn to my oncology appointment. I wasn't myself as I didn't know which way to turn. Understandably, I had a lot of anxiety and didn't know how to cope. I was praying to God but not yet fully depending on Him. I was looking for a quick fix, something that would cure me or help fight the cancer. I remembered everything I heard about marijuana. In my crazy frame of mind, I thought I found my cure, so I decided to get a lot of it right away.

The last time I smoked marijuana I was in my late teens. I called my older son and told him to buy me whatever I needed to get rid of the cancer, so he did. I smoked some marijuana and although it took a lot of my anxiety away, it only lasted a little while. The next day I decided to try an edible form of it, a chocolate candy bar. It tasted disgusting, but I didn't care. I shoved it down my throat anyway. As I was eating it, I didn't feel any different so I kept shoving more into my mouth. I waited a few more minutes and wasn't feeling any different, so I ate more. It began to take affect about a half hour later, and oh my, it was bad. It was the worst feeling in the world. I thought it would relax me, but it did the opposite. I went into a complete panic and became paranoid.

I wanted it out of my system so I asked my husband what I should do. He didn't have an answer for me so I came up with my own idea. I thought if I went into the jacuzzi, I could sweat it out. I was wrong. It made it worse. The hot water relaxed my body to the point where my legs gave out. I didn't realize my legs weren't functioning until I tried to get out of the jacuzzi. Now I was really panicking. My husband had gone to bed, and I didn't have my cell phone with me. I calmed myself down and focused on getting out. It took me about ten minutes to get out and into the house because my legs were very wobbly. I was so scared, and I couldn't wait for the feeling to end.

As soon as I got into the house, I called my son immediately and told him what happened. He laughed and told me that I had overdosed, but I couldn't die from eating edibles and not to worry, it would wear off in time. I couldn't believe what I was hearing. My son just told me that I overdosed. It was an experience I will never ever try again.

The next day, as my mind was still scrambling, I knew I

had to get my thoughts straightened out and to get myself together. I asked myself a question, "Anna, do you want to live,
or do you want to die?" I answered my own question and said
"I want to live!"

In the meantime, quite a few people were asking me if I
had heard about a famous preacher on television. I didn't
know who he was, and I had never seen his program. About
two days after overdosing on edibles, I received a phone call.
It was a lady that I didn't know and had never met. It was a
business call, but the crazy thing about her calling me was
that she asked me a silly question. While we were talking, I
told her I wasn't working at the moment because I was just
diagnosed with breast cancer. She asked me if I watched that
particular preacher on television that others had asked me
about. I couldn't believe it. When I hung up the phone with
her, I looked up and told God, "Okay, I got the hint." Right at
that moment, I turned on the TV, searched for his shows, and
recorded them.

From the very first time I sat down to watch his program,
he instantly became my new obsession. I watched him multiple times a day. I thank God for using this preacher to help
me. My faith became so much stronger every day. I quickly
learned how to completely lean and depend on God. I surren-
dered to Him and put my life in His hands. It's mind blowing
to me that, although I didn't see the point in her calling me at
the time, I now know that God put her in my path to help
save my life. I found that God truly uses every situation for
His glory. He always has a purpose.

"For I know the plans I have for you," declares the Lord, "plans to prosper you and not to harm you, plans to give you hope and a future" (Jeremiah 29:11).

TWO

So Many Decisions

It was finally time for my first oncology appointment. My husband, sister, and friend went with me for support. I'm so thankful they did because they took notes. I didn't hear much of what the doctor was saying because my mind just wasn't functioning normally. From my first appointment to the last, I didn't listen to most of what my doctors said about my cancer or my treatment.

You're probably wondering how it was possible not to listen when I was sitting in the same room as the doctor with the doctor speaking directly to me. Well, I had learned, at an early age, how to tune things out. There were seven of us in my family, all living in a thirteen hundred square foot home. My older brother played the drums in his bedroom, but I rarely heard him playing. If I hadn't developed this skill of tuning him out, I wouldn't have been able to watch television. That being said, I guess I chose to hear what I wanted to hear. As I am writing this, I realize that God was training my ears to tune things out at a young age because He knew one day it was going to help me get through the worst days of my life. He is so incredibly amazing!

I felt an instant connection and was very impressed with the first oncologist. She was easy to talk to and very compassionate, but I felt I needed a second opinion. To be honest, my initial response was that I didn't need a second opinion, but my family and friends talked me into it. As before, they went with me and took notes. After my first appointment and preparing for the next, I prayed and asked God to help me with my decision and to choose the best doctor for my treatment.

As soon as I arrived to get my second opinion and entered the building, I knew right then and there that it wasn't the right place for me. I felt a very strong, uneasy feeling. I have a lot of inner gut feelings, which I now know is discernment. God points me in the right direction every time I listen; and if I don't, I regret it. I wanted to turn around and leave, but I didn't because we had just driven quite a distance.

Before my second opinion appointment, I was asked to fill out paperwork. I didn't mind because paperwork is always part of the process, but this was different. We were called into a small office, and I was asked a bunch of questions. One of the questions was if I wanted to donate my body to science. I wanted to scream at her and leave the room, but I didn't want to make a scene so I just told her no. I couldn't believe they made me sign a waiver that I had declined the donation. I heavily disliked that place, as it had a very negative vibe. If I had known they were calling me into that room to have that conversation, I would have never gone in. To my surprise, this place was supposed to be the number one cancer treatment center in the world. Maybe, but not for me! At that point I knew I wasn't ever going back because I felt they actually expected me to die.

We had sat for hours waiting for this appointment so it was very frustrating, and yet I had my answer so quickly. But it wasn't over. As we walked down the hall to the patient room, I was dreading my consultation because I already knew I wouldn't be back. My friend brought the notes she took from the first appointment to compare with this appointment. The second oncologist read the notes and agreed to do the exact same treatment, except she said I would get very sick. This was contradictory to the first oncologist who said I wouldn't. Between the feeling that they were already preparing for my death and the doctor telling me I'd get sick, my decision was confirmed. I ended up with the best oncologist in the world, and I thank God for leading me to her.

After choosing my oncologist, it was time for my first appointment. That appointment took all day. When I arrived at my appointment, the technician who looked at my breast scans said they were bad and fuzzy. She had me redo my mammogram with her but this time in high definition. She showed me the difference between a high definition mammogram and the one that I had originally taken. It was shocking how clear her image was. Nowadays they do 3D mammograms, which I highly recommend, along with an ultrasound. I believed in my doctor, who took the original mammogram, to take great care of me, and I trusted my results. A lesson learned for all of us.

Even though it was really hard to tell if there was cancer in my breast in the original imaging, there was a strong possibility that my cancer grew after my original mammogram. I had a very aggressive cancer, and it could have grown to a stage three within those few months after my testing. I will never know.

After my doctor viewed my ultrasound and discussed my symptoms, she wouldn't let me leave until I did more testing. One of the tests was a Fish test, which is a test that determines exactly what type of cancer I had. They told us to hope for the best and hope for it to be HER2. I had everyone praying the test would come back HER2. I couldn't stop praying and hoping it wasn't worse. My mind was already overwhelmed, but waiting for the results put me over the edge because I'm very impatient. I was absolutely miserable!

It was nice that I felt I was on everyone's prayer chain, and it was a comfort to know so many people that I'd never met were praying for me. My prayer chain traveled through the city, county, state, and then to other countries. Thanks to God that through the power of prayer, the test result didn't come back HER2, it came back even better. I couldn't believe it! I was so relieved but mostly thankful.

I quickly learned how powerful prayer really is. I've always heard the expression, "There is power in prayer," but now that I experienced my prayers being answered, it's no longer just a saying to me. It's a personal experience—my personal experience. The words that I took for granted have so much power. What an unbelievable and amazing gift! Thank you, God, for giving us Your name, and what a powerful name it is!

After going through so much stress waiting for the Fish test results, I quickly decided I didn't want to know anything else about my cancer. I mean nothing! I put a stop to it immediately, and I told my friends and family that I didn't want to know because knowing would cause more stress and anxiety. I'm sure they were surprised and couldn't understand my decision, but they respected it. I never, not once, became curious about my type of cancer, and I never searched the internet about it. I chose not to know because it made me not feel like myself. It wasn't me, and I wanted me back. I needed to bring out that strong and positive person that I had always been. I knew I needed to change my frame of mind and to let go of all the stress and anxiety. Once I made the decision, a weight was lifted off my shoulders. I knew my thoughts were very critical to my well being so I protected them the only way I knew how by not listening or knowing how bad it really was.

To this day I can't even tell you what type of chemotherapy treatment I had. What I do know is that I had inflammatory breast cancer. It was in my lymph nodes, and it was stage three. It's always surprising to others who ask me about my treatment that I don't know the details about it. I tell them that I didn't pay any attention to my treatment because it was the only way I knew how to get through it. I can tell when someone doesn't understand my reasoning simply by the expression on their face. No, I wasn't in denial. It was how I chose to deal with it. It worked for me to focus on my faith and my inner strength. Ignoring any negativity or doubt strengthened me. The culmination of all these things kept my stress at bay.

Not only did I choose not to listen, I chose not to take prescription drugs on a regular basis. I understand and respect other women's decisions if they choose to take prescription drugs, but I chose not to. That was one way I felt I could keep my mind clear, focused, and in control.

I strongly believe a person's negative thoughts can encourage weakness. I needed to focus on getting myself mentally and physically strong enough for the fight of my life.

And I did! Once I did this, my relationship with God began to get stronger. God quickly became my everything. I prayed for Him to heal me and I promised Him I would help other women with breast cancer. I thanked Him for my healing, and I truly believed He would. I held God so close every second of the day, and He became my entire focus. I learned to completely trust Him because I didn't have a choice not to. I put my cancer and my life completely into His hands.

My friends and family couldn't believe how good I looked and how well I was doing, but it was all God and He gets all the credit. It wouldn't have been possible for me to hold myself together the way I did if God wasn't by my side, consistently holding me up.

I have been to several doctors in my lifetime, but my oncologist was exactly the one I needed for the time I needed her. God knew I needed her. I felt she completely understood and respected both me and my faith. And she kept her promise—I never got sick!

I recently received a letter in the mail that she was moving out of the country with her family. I cried and my heart was sad for days because it really felt like a death. I've always appreciated her, and throughout my battle, I told her over and over again that she was the best doctor in the world. I guess I didn't fully realize how much she meant to me until I heard she was leaving. She was so instrumental to my survival. She helped me feel secure, and her positivity made me that much stronger. I made an appointment so I could say goodbye. It was the first time that I cried in the patient room.

During my final appointment, she mentioned that I should get my blood work checked every three months with another oncologist whom she highly recommended. I looked at her with surprise, and I reminded her that I was healed and that she had told me at my previous appointment that my blood work was excellent. She then asked me if I was refusing treatment. Hearing those words shocked me. I didn't know what to say, so I told her I wasn't. I guess I was rejecting the treatment but not the recommendation. Ultimately, I told her that I would get my blood work done once a year as I always had done in the past. I knew she wasn't too happy with my decision, but I also knew it was protocol for her to ask.

She also asked me if I wanted to get a full body scan to have a clean bill of health. I thanked her and told her I didn't need another scan to tell me that the cancer was gone. I don't think or worry about my cancer ever coming back because I was healed. Between God, my positive outlook, and my brilliant doctor, there was no way I was ever going to lose my battle. It was impossible.

I can do all this through Him who gives me strength (Philippians 4:13).

THREE

It's Just Hair!

When I began preparing for chemotherapy, the thought of losing my long, thick beautiful hair was a tough one for me. I was really sad. It had taken me years to grow my hair out to the length it was, which was halfway down my back. Let's just say I was kind of attached to it. I loved my long hair. What in the world would I look like with short hair? Or no hair?

While I was at my doctor's appointment, I learned about cold cap therapy where you wear a cap during chemotherapy treatment to keep your hair from falling out. However, it's not a guarantee, and it's very expensive. When I got home from my doctor's appointment, I shared the information with my husband. He laughed and joked, and being the quick witted, practical man that he was, told me that I was going to have to go bald because it was too expensive. He felt that with all the medical bills we would be accumulating, it just wasn't something we could afford. I was disappointed for a while, but I eventually gave in.

As my realization of losing my hair grew, one thing I

knew for certain: I wasn't going to watch it fall out—not even one strand! There was no way I would put myself through unnecessary emotional trauma. That was it. I first decided that I would shave my head to a half inch in length before my first chemo treatment. I then chose to go from a shaved head to a completely bald head, and in hindsight, I felt that was exactly the right decision.

It was time for some shopping. I wanted to be ready to cover my bald head right away. I bought lots of different colored hats and beanies. I'm not a hat person. I never liked how I looked in hats, so I never wore them. Even though I bought multiple beanies and hats, I ended up wearing one black hat.

I wore that black hat every day and with every outfit. And I wore it proudly. It made me look and feel more like me. I lived my life in my black hat the same way I live my life today—full of joy and thanksgiving. I thank God He created a confident woman who always walks with her head held high. When people were rude and stared at me (and they stared a lot), or maybe it just felt like they stared a lot, I didn't care. I just stared back.

I was hesitant to buy a wig. They are expensive, and I felt like it might make me look sick or maybe make me look like somebody I wasn't. I didn't want to look different, not for everybody else but for me. Then, I thought of my boys and that maybe I should wear a wig while I was out in public with them. I should have discussed it with them before I spent five hundred dollars on something I was dreading to wear and only ended up wearing twice for a few hours.

My boys didn't care one bit about the wig. In fact, they liked me in my hat better. I think the wig made my boys feel uncomfortable because it made me look so different. I tried to get hair that looked close to mine, but it just wasn't the same.

Before I shaved my head, it was very important that I take some current pictures of me and my boys with my long hair. I believed my hair might never get that long again. And if or when it did grow to the length it once was, it probably wouldn't be for many years. I already had a great hair picture with my husband that we had taken in Las Vegas a couple months prior to my diagnosis. The boys and I ended up taking a lot of hair pictures, but my boys got frustrated as most teenage boys do when it comes to us moms taking pictures. At the time, taking those pictures meant the world to me. I had to have them. It's ironic because I'm not sure how I feel about them today. Every time I look at them, it reminds me of how I didn't want to let go. The pictures really don't mean as much to me as I thought they would.

Of course, being me and on a never-ending emotional roller coaster, I had another impulsive idea. I wanted my boys to help shave my head. Seems crazy now, but it didn't then. I wanted us to embrace my shaved head together. I felt it would give us a powerful moment and help us commemorate my journey. I truly thought they would be honored to do it, but boy was I wrong. They both refused. I asked them why, and they both said they just didn't want to, so I didn't continue to push the issue like I normally would have. I'm sure it was probably more than what they could handle since they were dealing with their own mixed emotions. Although I was a bit disappointed, it ended up to be a blessing in disguise.

Everything was moving so quickly. I decided to donate my hair to children. If I had gone with my original plan of letting the boys shave my head, then I wouldn't have followed through with my hair stylist. She knew exactly what to do and followed the protocol for a hair donation. Because they didn't shave it, I was able to properly prepare my hair for donation to a child in need. If my boys would have shaved my head, my hair would have been all over the floor and probably eventually in the trash. God is so good, and He knows what's best. I know He stopped my boys from shaving my head. I believe that He had a particular child He was going to bless who needed my hair.

After making my decision to have it professionally cut, I called my hair stylist and broke the news to her. She was so kind and told me she would come to my home instead of me going to the salon. I tried my best to mentally prepare myself before she came over. I kept telling myself, *It's just hair and it will grow back*. No matter what I told myself, I still didn't want to do it, and I grew increasingly anxious. Who knew one could be so attached to hair? I just needed to find the courage and that's what I did. I began to focus on the donation, and this really helped my thought process during such a difficult time.

I asked a good friend to help me with the donation, and she handled everything for me. When my hair stylist walked into my home, it became so real. I was very nervous but I didn't cry. In fact, I never cried about losing my hair. I just didn't want to let go. It was a real struggle for me, and I was super sad but it was time. I had a stool set up in my kitchen, and I took a deep breath (well, actually a few deep breaths) and told myself it was only temporary. It would grow back.

My stylist draped the cape around me and sectioned my hair into ponytails so she could cut them off properly for the donation. It was the most devastating sound ever to hear the scissors cutting through my ponytails. To this day I can still hear the sound of those scissors. One by one, she handed each ponytail to my friend who then put them into an envelope. I just kept visualizing a child being so excited to have hair again. It brought a smile to my face. I sure wish I could see a picture of that child.

Once she finished cutting off all of the ponytails, she plugged in the hair clippers. As she started shaving my head, I began to slowly embrace it because I didn't have a choice not to. To my surprise, by the time she was finished, I was emotionally okay. Maybe because I couldn't change it, and it was over or maybe just because. When it was time for me to look in the mirror, I was kind of scared. When I looked, it wasn't as bad as I thought it would be, except for my hair color. My long hair was dark brown and now my extremely short hair was salt and pepper. Wow, I have never been so thankful for hair dye. Other than looking ten years older with my new salt and pepper hair, I was pleasantly surprised of how I looked with a shaved head. Shortly after, the anticipation and apprehension was over, and I was relieved. I accepted my temporary new look, and I was proud of myself for being so brave.

Once I started my treatment, I had a different outlook about losing my hair. I was so glad I didn't try saving my hair through the cooling treatment. l felt my hair would have been full of poison and chemicals, another hindsight to be thankful for. Once it started to grow again, it was new, soft, and healthy hair. It's terrible to think of what I put myself through because I didn't want to let go of my hair. Today, my hair is growing back slowly but exactly the same—thick and wavy. And yes I'm still thankful for hair dye. I thank God for always knowing what's best for me. He knew I would be happier with all new healthy hair. I will keep saying this: He is an awesome God!

I'd been through the hair loss so I wasn't worried or sad about my eyebrows and eyelashes falling out. I'm very hairy by nature and I have thick eyebrows so I figured they would grow back quickly, which they did. My eyebrows stayed throughout most of my treatment. They were a lot thinner than normal, but they held on until a month before my treatment ended.

A couple of days before my first chemo treatment, I was offered free eyebrow tattooing from a tattoo artist who works for my plastic surgeon. The artist just started offering free, temporary eyebrow tattooing to breast cancer patients who would be losing their eyebrows during treatment. I couldn't believe it, and I said yes immediately. In fact, I was her very first patient, and I became the face of her promotion. Since I was her first patient, she also tattooed the inner top of my eyelids but that is permanent tattooing and to this day I love it. Because of the permanent tattooing, when my eyelashes fell out, my eyes had color. They didn't look naked. It was one of the best decisions I made. Once my eyebrows fell out, I still had the shape, and they looked so good. I didn't feel like I looked like all the other chemo patients. Her gift helped me through a most challenging time. What a blessing! God provided everything at just the right time, every time.

Chemo does have a positive side effect: the hair on the rest of my body also eventually fell out. I actually liked the way it looked. It didn't bother me not to have hair in those places. I loved the fact that I didn't have to shave for a while, because normally I have to shave every other day. I was hoping it wouldn't grow back, but it did.

It's Just Hair!

And even the very hairs of your head are all numbered (Matthew 10:30).

FOUR

The Nightmare Is Real

What I was experiencing felt like a bad nightmare. Most of us have woken up from a bad dream, only to feel relieved when we realize the dream wasn't real. Well, this bad nightmare was real, and there would be no waking up for a while.

When I was first diagnosed with cancer, I wanted to start chemo right away. I wanted the cancer out of my body immediately. That's ironic because when it was finally time to start my treatment, I didn't want to do it. The unknown was scary for me. Not knowing what to expect or how the chemo was going to make me feel made me anxious, and at times, my chest felt heavy. I never said to myself that I was afraid, but I was feeling the fear. I tried to mentally prepare myself, but it's impossible to prepare for the unknown. I couldn't wrap my mind around it, so I prayed and I prayed. I put a Bible verse on my refrigerator and constantly read it out loud.

Do not fear, for I am with you; do not be dismayed, for I am your God. I will strengthen you and help you; I will uphold you with my righteous right hand (Isaiah 41:10).

I must have read that verse a thousand times, and I held onto and trusted in those words during my entire journey.

One thing I decided to get before I began chemo was genetic testing. I did it for the sake of my boys and for my sisters. Genetic testing is a blood test that helps determine whether a person has inherited a gene that may increase their risk of certain cancers. If my results would have come back positive, my boys and sisters would have had a fifty percent chance of getting breast cancer in their lifetime. Praise God, it came back negative!

My mom's sister had breast cancer about forty years earlier so I thought for sure my test results would come back positive. I have learned that only a small percent of breast cancer is hereditary, and when I really think about it, that makes me sad. And it makes me wonder what is going on in and around our bodies to produce this cancer! Is it something we are eating? Is it something we aren't eating? Is it in the air we breathe? Is it something we are or aren't doing?

I couldn't stop wondering. I started to think of habits that I had over a long period of time. I had taken cholesterol medicine for thirteen years, and I had used sunblock on my face daily for about twenty years prior to my diagnosis. I wasn't going to take any chances, so I continued to control my cholesterol with pills that help support my heart. However, I did change my sunblock to a safer one that doesn't have as many chemicals. I don't know if this will make much of a difference, but it makes me feel better that I'm making better choices.

Since my breast cancer wasn't hereditary, that meant my body produced it itself. I've learned there is just no rhyme or reason why people get breast cancer. I hope there will come a day when medical research figures out exactly why so many of us have to fight this battle.

Even though my genetic results came back negative, I didn't feel it gave me complete peace of mind. I believe my boys are still at risk so I talked to them about giving themselves breast exams at least once a month. I'm sure they feel invincible, as I did at their age, and they probably don't do it, but I do hope they take this seriously. I feel good knowing I shared this information with them, and I pray for them all the time.

The morning of my first chemotherapy treatment finally arrived. My husband drove me to the hospital to have a port put into my chest. The doctor recommended an implantable port that goes under the skin and is used for chemo infusions and blood withdrawals. It was a bizarre device. Every time a nurse hooked me up for my infusions or to take blood it released a horrible taste in my mouth. I found myself popping a mint or lifesaver into my mouth every time to help disguise the taste.

As usual, I didn't know what to expect, and the port ended up being very painful for months. I asked my doctor if the pain would subside, and she said the pain may be caused from the port sitting on a nerve. I contemplated having it removed, but then my injections would be administered directly into my arms and I was told the veins could collapse. I wasn't going to take that chance and did my best to ignore the pain and prayed.

After my port was implanted, we were off to my first treatment. Two of my girlfriends met us there and sat with us in the waiting room. I kept a brave face but inside I felt like I couldn't handle what was about to happen. I was petrified. I could have put myself into a complete panic and hyper-ventilated but I didn't let myself. Every time I heard the door open and a nurse was about to call a name, my anxiety level went up. When they finally called my name, I wanted to run the other way. As I started to walk my very first long walk down the hallway to the infusion room, I asked God to hold my hand. I closed my hand tightly, and I imagined Him holding my hand while we walked there together. I know He was with me because I couldn't have done that walk without Him. When the walk ended, I opened my hand to let go of His and thanked Him for walking with me.

There were multiple chairs in the room so I chose a chair and sat down. I couldn't stop praying and thanking God for being with me. Then I told my body to stay strong. I wasn't aware that I couldn't have too many people with me at these appointments, and as I mentioned before my girlfriends had met us there. They actually booted my husband out of the room. He is so easy going and didn't even care. It was very comforting that my friends were with me. It's what I needed at that particular appointment, and they knew it, he knew it, and most of all, God knew it. My husband did, however, sit with me during every chemo treatment thereafter.

Before every chemo infusion, the nurse told me that they had to draw my blood to make sure all of my levels were normal. If the results were abnormal, I couldn't get my infusion that day. I looked up at the nurse and told her my levels would be normal every time because I had faith in a big God. She said, "Well, I still have to let you know that they might not always come back normal." I told her again that I would be fine. I was dead serious, and I think she thought I was a little crazy. I can only imagine the conversations the nurses had behind closed doors about us patients. I wanted to set a precedent because this was our first conversation and I wouldn't accept any negativity, not even from my nurses. After a while, the nurses got to know me and how important my faith was. I came to find out there were a couple of nurses who had a personal relationship with God just like me.

Once they were finished hooking me up to start my infusion, I would always quietly pray. Then, I would say God's name to keep the enemy away from me and out of the room. And I always reminded Satan he would never win. I also told the chemo that it would not damage my body, and that God was in control. The Christian nurses bowed their heads and agreed in prayer with me every time. It was awesome. Thanks to God, my blood levels came back in the normal range every single time.

My five months of chemo began. From the very first time I sat in the chair, I kept my feet on the floor. The nurses would ask if I wanted to lay back or if I needed a pillow. I always refused no matter how uncomfortable I was. Sometimes I did accept a blanket because my legs got cold, but I sat with my feet on the floor every appointment for several hours. Most everyone else in the room made themselves as comfortable as they could and laid back in their chair with a pillow and a blanket. I never laid back and rested while chemo entered my body because I felt that would be a sign of weakness. I wasn't going to give in and let it win. I never once took my feet off the ground while I was getting my infusion. For months God and I sat strong and in control while the chemo was going through my veins. I had to prove in every way possible that He and I would win. I sat and listened to worship music and talked to other patients while my husband worked on his computer until my infusion was finished.

The first two months of my treatment were the most aggressive. I had two different infusions: one was injected from a drip bag and the other one was injected by hand. The one injected by hand was a red liquid. I guess I hadn't made it clear enough to the first nurse that I wasn't going to accept negativity. When I saw the liquid I said to the nurse, "That's weird, it's red," and she replied, "People refer to it as the devil's blood." My eyes widened and I about jumped out of my seat. I told the nurse, "There is no way that anything called the devil's blood is going into my veins, so I'm calling it God's blood." Believe it or not she laughed and agreed with me. I think she finally got me.

I felt such relief after my first treatment because the fear of the unknown was gone. I was drained but not as badly as I thought I would. It took a couple of infusions to really feel the effect of the chemo. After my anxiety of the unknown went away, my confidence and courage started to become stronger. It didn't take long for me to realize *I got this!* The chemo caused me to feel exhausted most of the time. I had little to no energy, didn't have an appetite, and I felt really nauseous. Although I never threw up, I still lost a lot of weight.

During a few weeks of my chemotherapy treatments, I also had to get shots of Neulasta. After my chemotherapy infusion, the nurse would tape the device to my stomach. The device was set to release a shot into my stomach a few hours after my treatment, and it would beep once it was completed. I knew that it was to help my blood cells, but I didn't know exactly what it was doing. When the release time neared, I sat on the couch until the treatment was over.

I learned that if I moved around, the side effects would be much easier to handle. When I laid down, it felt like something was taking over my body and I felt paralyzed. This overwhelming and very scary feeling made it seem like I couldn't move. I didn't feel as if I were in control, so I had to get on my feet. When I realized it felt better to move around, I did just that. I slowly got out of bed and walked around, and I knew I needed to keep moving for that awful, intense feeling to subside.

At my next infusion appointment, I asked other women who were also getting this shot if they were having the same experience. An elderly lady told me she didn't feel a difference but another lady, who was closer to my age, told me she was having the same experience. I dreaded getting those shots, but I told myself *It must be doing something positive for me so be thankful it was invented.* I tried to stay as positive as possible, and I constantly prayed.

In my personal opinion, the worst side effect from the chemo was how it affected my brain. It was dreadful. I was in what is called a chemo fog. Sometimes I felt extremely miserable and couldn't remember anything. If I watched a movie, the next day I couldn't remember much about it or even how it ended. Oh it was so frustrating! Today, I am much more forgetful. I feel my poor memory might be from all of the chemotherapy treatments, but it also very well might be from my older age or maybe a little mixture of both. Either way, I'm in God's hands.

After a few weeks of my treatments, I had a migraine that lasted for almost two weeks. For those of you who experience migraines, I feel your pain. Along with my migraine, I experienced vertigo. My migraine got so bad that I had to go to a specialist to get meds. Having a migraine and dealing with a chemo fog brain at the same time were extremely difficult. I was in complete misery, but I stayed as strong as possible. Those were the worst days of my battle.

At one of my treatments I noticed my hands and feet were feeling warm and somewhat painful so during my chemo treatment the nurse put ice packs under my feet and on my hands. I learned that chemo doesn't go to cold places in your body. Shortly after I finished with my five months of treatment, all of those symptoms slowly went away, thank God. Those were the only major side effects that happened during my chemo treatments.

Throughout my treatment, I didn't have any caffeine and hardly any sugar. I've always loved sugar, my biggest weakness. Today, I try my best to keep sugar to a minimum, which is really hard for me. To be honest, some days are better than others. I also used to drink a lot of soda for the caffeine, but now that habit is gone. I like the fact of waking up in the morning and not feeling groggy. My only caffeine exception is chocolate, and there is no way I'm giving that up. Do you blame me?

I basically ate just enough to keep up my strength, which was very little. Nothing ever sounded good because my taste buds had been tainted from the chemo, and I always had a weird taste in my mouth. Drinking water never bothered me, so I was able to keep myself hydrated. I didn't pay much attention to the amount of weight I was losing because it was the last thing on my mind. Once I completed my treatments and I started to feel better, I realized my weight loss. I don't know the exact amount of weight I lost, but it was a lot. I loved the way I looked, especially in my clothes. And my face was thinner too. The last time I was around that weight I was in my twenties. Strangely, when I looked in the mirror it reminded me of my sickness because that's not how I looked before I got sick. It became a mental issue because I didn't lose the weight on my terms. As I started to feel better, I began to eat more and more so I started to slowly gain the weight back. I've been slightly overweight most of my life so I didn't mind the weight gain because I started to feel like myself again. Today, I have gained all the weight back. Kind of a bummer because now I need to lose at least twenty pounds. At least it will be on my terms.

God healed me and I needed to start taking better care of my body. It was this realization that prompted me to stop eating meat after my treatment ended because meat is full of hormones. I wasn't substituting the proper proteins that my body needed, and I felt tired from the lack of iron so now I eat a small amount every day. I try my best to only eat organic meats, fruits, and vegetables.

The last day of my treatment was such a happy day, and I was so excited. It is a sobering thought to think how happy I was to get my last infusion, even though it kicked my butt. Just knowing it was going to be over forever made me happy. I am so proud of myself for being so strong and brave through the worst days of my life. Thank you, God, for holding me!

> *For I am the Lord your God who takes hold of your right hand and says to you, Do not fear; I will help you* (Isaiah 41:13).

FIVE

Power of Positivity

No matter what life throws at me, I tell myself it could be worse! There is always something to be thankful for. Once I decided to completely rely on God, not only did my faith become stronger but so did my body and my mind. I never really thought I could get any stronger but all of me became increasingly stronger once I started to speak out loud to myself. I may not have looked like her, but I sure felt like Wonder Woman.

One day I felt a prompting to dig deep and bring out my inner strength. I had to get my body and mind ready to fight like I had never fought before. This was a battle for my life, and I was going to fight with every fiber of my being. I began speaking to myself in a strong and authoritative voice. I would tell myself how strong and amazing I was. I put my hands in a fist, closed my eyes tight, held my head up high, and threw my arms up in the air as if I had just won a race. I spoke to my entire body and praised it. I always spoke to my brain first and told it how strong and powerful it was. Then, I would tell it how proud I was of it for keeping my body so strong and how we could do anything with God.

Then, I spoke individually to all my organs. I spoke to my heart, lungs, liver, and kidneys. I continued to speak to my intestines, blood cells, bones, muscles, and even my tissues. I told each of them how strong they were and to keep fighting together and to support each other. I also told them how extremely proud I was of them for working together and for staying so strong and healthy. I did this at least once a day throughout my entire journey.

On the days of my chemo infusions, I told my body that the chemo was coming and that we could do this with God by our side so to keep fighting. I always reminded my body that this wasn't forever. It was only temporary.

After I spoke to my body and praised it, I spoke directly to the cancer. I spoke very aggressively and in a firm tone because that's what it deserved. While I would look down at my breast, I would point my finger directly at the cancer and scold it. I told it, "You are not going to win." I told it that I didn't accept it, and it was going to get crushed by the power of God's blood. I told it that it meant nothing to me. I spoke to it as if it had feelings, and I wanted to hurt it. Sometimes I even referred to it as a cold because colds go away.

I always ended by thanking God for putting His blood through my body and for keeping me healthy. I thanked Him over and over again, every day, for seven months, before it actually happened.

My faith and relationship with God grew stronger each day. All of my life I've loved Him, but it wasn't until I decided to completely relinquish everything and rely on Him that I learned so much more about my faith. I had to learn how to completely trust Him, and it was tough. I would put my life into His hands and then take it back and then do that all over again. It was a constant battle, but I learned to leave my life in His hands because I really didn't have any other choice. I couldn't have made it through one minute of my journey without Him.

Knowing everything happens for a reason, I didn't need to know why this happened to me. I just needed to remember it was all part of God's plan. He knew even before He formed me in my mother's womb. "Before I formed you in the womb I knew you" (Jeremiah 1:5a).

We usually don't have a choice in what happens to us. Sometimes God reveals His reasons why and sometimes He doesn't. It is pretty incredible to watch His plan unfold. It truly amazes me.

Talking out loud to myself and keeping myself in control brought me tremendous strength. As each day went by, I became stronger and stronger. Nothing could stop God and me. We were victorious. His strength continued to shine through me.

My visitors would tell me that they didn't expect me to act the way I did. They thought I would be laying down or resting on the couch. I rarely laid down to rest as I felt that was a sign of weakness or that I was giving in. The only time I rested was when I felt like my body just couldn't do anymore. I did occasionally get to a point where I couldn't function because I was pushing myself so hard. I lived my days as normal as possible and tried my best to ignore any feelings of defeat.

During my aggressive treatments, I went to work for a few days but only for a few hours. One morning before work, I was drained and my mind was in a complete chemo fog, but

I got myself ready, threw my wig on, and continued the day as if nothing were wrong. Even though my mind was not functioning correctly, I continued to work.

One of my favorite things to do was to get away with my friends and/or my family. I went on several weekend get-aways and one of the most difficult things I learned, after several trips away, was that I couldn't be in the sun. I didn't always tell my doctor what I was doing or where I was going, but at one of my visits I told her that I was going to Lake Havasu for the weekend. She told me to stay out of the sun, and I am so grateful I chose to tell her because I would have never known. At that visit I learned that certain forms of chemotherapy can make the skin more sensitive to the sun. It was summertime and being in the sun was not the best place for me to be, but at least I got to be with my family and friends. Sometimes I couldn't go outside to do what everyone else was doing, but being present was extremely important to my healing process.

Throughout the day, I always reminded myself how strong I was. I said it out loud regardless of who was around me. My friends and family may have thought I was a little nutty, but I didn't care. The worse I felt, the more I would say it. I felt it was a mental battle. I kept my mind extremely strong every minute of the day. It's truly unbelievable to think how much strength we have when we really need it. I didn't have a choice not to believe how unbelievably strong my mind and body really were. God was in control, not the cancer or the chemo.

From the beginning to the end of my battle, my boys only heard positive words come out of my mouth. Not once did they hear "What if?" No matter how I felt or how I looked, I told them I was going to be fine because I knew I would be.

One night I was resting on the recliner because it was one of my hard days, and I felt lifeless and my oldest son sat on the couch across from me.

He said, "Mom, what if you get worse?"

I told him, "If I'm not going there, neither are you."

He said, "Okay."

We had a great conversation, and I reassured him that I was going to be fine because I was in God's hands.

I kept a smile on my face regardless of how I felt. There were days I felt I could barely move or get out of bed because the chemo was sucking the life out of me. One morning while I was laying in bed, I felt so weak I said to myself, *I have to get up and get on my feet.* With every ounce of strength that I had, I rolled myself out of bed and spoke out loud to the cancer, reminding it that it wasn't going to win. I had to prove to the cancer once again that we would win. When I finally got to my feet, I thanked God for all His help and for giving me His strength.

I may have looked like a chemo patient to some people, but that isn't how I saw myself. I didn't see myself any different than I do today. It wasn't denial. I knew exactly what I was going through. I just saw myself as a beautiful bald woman, not a sick woman. I never dwelled on the fact that I had cancer. I never asked *Why me?* I never thought *What if I die?* Not once! If negativity tried to creep into my mind, I would get rid of it right away. I think negativity is a sign of weakness and defeat. It represents failing. Between my powerful mind and my powerful God, what could come against me? Nothing!

During this time I didn't take pictures of myself. It was

not a time that I wanted to remember because it was a time in my life I didn't want to look back on. It's tough in this day and age, which is so social media driven, when we want to document all of our events through pictures. I told my friends not to take any pictures of me because I didn't want my pictures posted on social media.

I did have three exceptions. The first was that I allowed my tattoo artist to take pictures of my progress throughout my journey for her project. I looked at those pictures months after I completed my chemo treatments, and I couldn't believe what I saw. I just couldn't believe that was me in the pictures. It was shocking. My face was very puffy, and I looked like a completely different person. When I looked in the mirror, that was not the person I saw. It seriously blew my mind because I never thought I had looked like a chemo patient.

The second exception was at my friend's fiftieth birthday dinner. Her mom loves to take pictures. She asked me to take a picture with my friend to document her birthday. At first I told her that I wasn't taking pictures at that time in my life, but then I gave in because she was so disappointed. I asked her not to post it on social media, and she agreed and proceeded to take the picture. I am very thankful she kept her word.

The third exception was in Las Vegas. We went to a concert, and I took a picture with my husband and a couple of friends. I didn't really want to take the picture, but I figured I would since I was dressed up and my makeup looked good. It turned out to be a really cute picture, and I was surprisingly happy with it. I didn't want to keep it, though, so I deleted it off my phone.

When I first was diagnosed with cancer, I told my friends and family I didn't want anything pink. I had never liked the color. I was more of a tomboy growing up. I played basketball and softball. Not once in my life did I own anything pink, at least as far back as I can remember. I am so thankful God gave me boys because I can't imagine having a daughter that would want a pink bedroom, especially at the time I was going through this trial. I will not wear anything pink, not even a pink ribbon.

I know pink ribbons mean so much to so many breast cancer survivors and supporters, and I respect that, but I see it as a reminder of my battle. I view the ribbon as giving the cancer unwanted attention. To me it goes hand in hand with not seeing myself as a chemo patient. I feel I don't need a pink ribbon to tell me I am strong or that I am a survivor. I already know I am. I don't like to look back, and I don't like the attention. It is in my past, and it is over.

It is a proven fact that chemo can do serious damage to your body, but I believe because of my positive attitude and God by my side, I had minimal issues. My body stayed strong because I spoke to it out loud all the time.

Be on your guard; stand firm in the faith; be courageous; be strong (1 Corinthians 16:13).

Six

The Importance of Support

My husband and my boys were and are my main support system. This wasn't just my battle; it was theirs too. I've been married for seventeen years. My husband is a kind man and a great provider. He took such great care of me throughout my journey, but he was most exceptional after my surgeries.

I've spoiled my family by always doing the cooking and most of the cleaning in our home. During this time, most nights I didn't have the energy to cook or to clean the house. My husband doesn't like to cook so my oldest son took on the responsibility and cooked for us most nights. All of them always made sure that I was okay, and they would frequently ask me if I needed anything. They kept the house clean the best they knew how, but they couldn't clean to my standards so I had to hire a housekeeper for a few months. I appreciated everything they did for me, and doing what they could meant the world to me.

My boys are seven years apart. My oldest son had moved out of the house a few months before I got diagnosed. I felt I needed to see all of them every day to get through my battle so I asked him to move back home and he did. I knew he really didn't want to, but he understood and he never made a fuss about it. Not only did I need to see them every day, but I needed to hug and kiss them to get myself through each day. My boys and husband have my heart, and they were and are my reason.

To my surprise, my extended family was a very small percent of my support system. To this day I don't understand why they chose not to help me much, and I don't think I ever will. We are a close family, and we spend a lot of time together. It was so hard for me to wrap my mind around it, and it hurt me so badly. The only way I was able to cope was to put it in the back of my mind and not think about it. I knew I could battle without them, but I didn't want to. I'm sure they have their reasons, but to be honest, they couldn't have given me one that would have been good enough. I have since forgiven them.

A couple days after I was diagnosed, I broke the news to my cousin who is like a sister to me. She told me she would help me and be by my side every step of the way. The next day, she came over to visit me. When she got to my house she told me she invited a few other people over. I wasn't happy about it, and I felt she should've asked me first. I wasn't in the mood to see anyone, and neither was my family. We weren't in a good place, understandably, and we didn't feel like entertaining visitors. We were barely functioning ourselves.

It was a really hard day because I felt the need to act as normal as possible, but I wasn't in my right frame of mind. Most everyone started to drink alcohol so their visit lasted throughout the evening. At times I wanted to scream. It wasn't a time to party. I knew everyone that came over meant well and I knew they loved me, but I was wondering why they were really there. I believed they came over because they felt it was the right or proper thing to do. It made them feel better. I knew it was impossible for most of them to empathize with me and to know what I was going through because they had never been in my shoes. It felt like they came over to say goodbye as if I were going to die.

For the most part, my family gets along really well. I have three sisters and my brother is in heaven with our mom and dad. I needed my sisters, and I thought they were going to be there for me more than they were. I especially wished that my mom could have been by my side. Before my healing, I cried for my mom because I missed her so much. I wanted her to hold me through my battle and tell me everything was going to be okay. Since I've been healed, I don't cry for her anymore. Knowing how happy she is with God makes me smile every time I think of her. "May the Lord keep watch between you and me when we are away from each other" (Genesis 31:49).

I'm sure it wasn't intentional, but I did get my feelings hurt a few times. There were promises made when I was first diagnosed that weren't followed through—promises to cook for us and to clean our home. I think it's important for people to know when you make a promise to someone, especially in their most vulnerable times, to follow through. At this time, in my extreme vulnerability, these broken promises cut me very deeply. Those who haven't gone through something like this don't truly understand. I came to terms with that, after spending many days in tears. In time I did get some help. More than tasks, as treatment progressed, I realized what I needed, was to know that my family and friends would be there for me no matter what.

As I continued to break the news to the rest of my family, I was hearing more and more negativity, and my feelings kept getting hurt. When I told my nephew, he told me that I needed to hurry up and travel with my family in case I died. What the heck? I told him I wasn't going to die, and he said, "You never know." If I could have jumped through the phone, I would have. Good thing we were on the phone because if he had been in front of me I would have hit him.

Throughout this entire experience, I learned that many people don't have social grace. Not because they are ignorant but because they just don't know what to say. How can they be empathetic when they haven't been through it? Many people don't think before they speak, at least that's what I experienced on a regular basis. I can't imagine saying anything negative to someone who is fighting for their life or could possibly die. The worst words I heard were, "Hope for the best and prepare for the worst." So unbelievable!

About nine days after my diagnosis, my cousin and I were at the market, and she suggested I start taking antidepressants. I told her that I wasn't going to take an antidepressant. She argued with my decision and told me that they have helped other friends with cancer, and they all took them so I needed to start taking them. She got really upset with me because I wasn't listening to her or doing things her way. In the middle of the store she started to yell at me, so I yelled back. I couldn't believe we were arguing in a grocery store and we continued to argue as we were checking out. It was embarrassing, but I stood my ground and in the end I won the argument. I never took any of those things.

I found myself upset every time we talked or texted, so I finally told her that she needed to stay out of my life until I was finished with my battle. It was very difficult for me to tell her, but I had to do what I had to do for my survival. I made it about me because quite honestly it was about me. Although I told her not to contact me, it still made me sad she never tried. I just couldn't believe that out of all the people in my life, I thought she was going to be the one who stuck by my side. Today we are talking again, and I forgave her because I love her.

Eventually there was so much hurt and negativity, I called my sister and asked her to put out a group text to the family, telling them that I didn't want any more phone calls, and I would call them when I was ready. When the phone stopped ringing, it gave me time to regroup. I didn't want any further drama so I had to put up boundaries. About time, right? I needed to stop thinking about the negative words that I was hearing. But the hardest part was getting over those painful words that I never thought I would hear from my family whom I love so much.

I have the greatest girlfriends in the world, and I couldn't have battled without them. They carried my stress amongst each other so I didn't have to worry about anything. They all knew that I didn't want to hear anything negative about my cancer, and they respected it. They stepped up and learned everything they felt they needed to know and shared with each other but never with me.

Since the cancer was in my lymph nodes, my doctors wanted to know if the cancer had traveled to other parts of my body. This required a PET scan, which is a full body scan. A few days after the scan, I picked up the results. My friend who took notes at my doctor's appointments lives an hour away. I usually gave her my test results when I would see her at my appointments. She wasn't at this appointment and felt she needed to read the PET scan results right away. The fastest way to get them to her was to take pictures on my phone and text them to her. As soon as I sent the results, I deleted the pictures. I never became curious or felt a need to read the results, and I never did.

I will never forget when she called me back to tell me the unbelievable news. I was putting groceries in my car when I answered the phone. The first thing she said was, "I can't believe it. Whatever you are doing, don't stop doing it." Then she continued telling me that the cancer had stayed in my chest, and it hadn't travelled to any other part of my body. I told her it was God. It was the best news I had heard, and I was so happy. I had the biggest smile on my face while I thanked God out loud in the parking lot. I knew He stopped my cancer from spreading throughout my body. He gets all the credit. He continued to watch over me and helped me every step of the way.

Each of my friends have their own strengths, and together they made a very strong support system. The same friend who lives an hour away went to most doctor's appointments with me and listened to the doctors because she knew I wasn't listening. She took notes and went home and googled them. At the next appointment, she always asked questions to clarify what she heard and studied. She put together a group text to keep all of my friends and family updated. After I did any type of testing, I gave her the results, and she would inform them.

Another amazing friend did my running around for me,

and she called me every day to see if I needed anything. If I did, she had it at my door within an hour. She was my worry wart, but my strength helped her become a stronger person so we will always be a blessing to each other. My other friends would visit me and keep in touch. They could never understand what I was going through, and I will never understand what I put them through. I appreciate them and love them more than they will ever know. I thank God every day that He placed them in my life. Once I was finished with my treatments, all of my closest girlfriends and my sister and I went away together for the weekend to celebrate because we had a big reason to celebrate!

The facility that I chose to go to for my treatment offers newly diagnosed women emotional support. They try to match women with the same type of cancer and treatments. About a week or so after I was diagnosed, I was offered support by the facility. I thought it would be nice to talk to someone who survived my type of cancer so I agreed to a phone call. It was out of my comfort zone to talk to a complete stranger about my personal life. I felt she knew what I was going through and how I was feeling so she could help me with support. We only spoke on the phone for about five minutes because I cut the conversation short. She was very nice, but I heard weakness in her voice; it really bothered me. I couldn't wait to hang up the phone because I felt stronger than her, and she was the survivor.

One day while I was in the reception area waiting to be called for my chemo treatment, a lady sat next to me. She asked how I was doing and if I needed to talk about anything. I thanked her but told her no and that I was fine. I appreciated her checking on me, but I heard so much pity in her voice.

She talked to me in a soft voice as if she were talking to a child. It made me squirm. I told her that I was a really strong person and that I leaned on God.

I didn't want to be bothered with any more unexpected visitors while I was waiting for my appointments so I asked the facilitator to remove my name from the support list. She was a little taken back that I asked such a request, but I felt stronger than these women, and I was!

During my chemo infusions, I had conversations with other breast cancer patients, and we all agreed on one thing: the friends and family we thought would be there weren't and vice versa. It was that one friend that we all least expected that became our everything. I have always had great people in my life and I still do, but when it comes down to the nitty gritty, it all changed.

From the beginning of my journey until the end, my church gave me tremendous support. The pastor of my church came to our home to pray with my family and I before I started my chemo treatments. I received weekly cards in the mail and members of the church brought my family and I dinner, which was so appreciated.

One Sunday, about a week and half after I was first diagnosed, my family and I went to meet with the elders of the church so they could pray over us before the morning service. We all gathered in the senior pastor's office and he asked me to tell everyone what was going on. I started to share what little I knew, that I had stage three breast cancer and it was in three of my lymph nodes. As soon as I said, "three of my lymph nodes," my husband blurted out, "No, it's in eleven!" I had no idea, and my mind started racing and I began to cry. I guess since my husband felt they were praying, they might as well know the whole truth. Talk about dropping a bomb! I couldn't stop crying so the pastor handed me tissues. It meant so much to me that my family and friends were gathered together while the elders and the pastor prayed over me.

When I was sitting in church before the service began, I opened my tissue and saw that most of the tissue was a light orange color. It scared me for a second because I didn't know why. Then I realized it was from the dye they had injected into me when I had the PET scan the day before. I started to laugh to myself because I could only imagine what the elders and pastor were thinking when they saw orange tears running down my face while we talked and prayed. I'm sure it must have freaked them out. I still laugh about it today because every time they see me they probably think *There's the lady with the orange tears*. The funniest part about it is that I never told them that it was the dye.

Not only did the elders and pastor pray for me, but so did so many other people at my church that I didn't even know. The staff put me on the prayer chain and in the weekly bulletin to keep everyone updated with my progress. I am so thankful for all the support and prayers that I received from my church during the time when I needed it most.

When I was a child my mother raised my siblings and me in the Catholic faith. Then one day, my brother walked down the street to get his hair cut. The stylist happened to be the pastor's wife at a Christian church, and she invited him to attend their church. He came home very excited and asked my mom if he could go, and she agreed. Soon after, we converted from Catholicism to Christianity, and we all gave our lives to God. I love the fact that my brother's visit to the barber changed our family's lives. It goes to show you that God works through us all. He is an amazing God!

My relationship with God began when I was a young teenager. It wasn't the greatest relationship, but I was learning about Him. As I grew a little older, my faith continued to grow but at a slow pace as I would continually put Him on the back burner. I was the typical teenager growing up in the eighties and nineties, going to clubs and concerts. I smoked and drank because I thought it was a cool thing to do.

My relationship with God was weak at best, and I didn't pray much. I wish I could go back and talk to my young self because I would sure have a lot to say. Knowing now that God was with me every step of the way and watching over me fills my heart with joy.

As I grew older, my personal relationship with Him was developing, and I began to pray more. Once I had my first son, I went to church a lot more so he could learn about Him too. And I'm sad to say, during that time I only worshipped Him while I was at church.

I'm so thankful I had my childlike faith to fall back on. I didn't really fully rely on Him until I was fighting for my life, which has led to the relationship with Him that I have today. I'm far from the perfect Christian. I sin like everyone else. Not even those closest to Jesus (His disciples) were perfect. They were sinners just like all of us.

I don't believe we should categorize God. People seem to think that their affiliation with their denomination makes them better. This tends to lead to judgment. God is a God of love. He loves us all regardless of our religious affiliation or preference.

I also know I don't have to be in church to worship Him. I love to worship Him by simply looking up and smiling because He makes me so happy. I also love to worship while I'm driving the car or cleaning my home. I feel anytime is a good time to worship Him. Having a personal relationship with Him and giving my life to Him is what matters the most. He knows my heart, and He knows He is my everything.

Not looking to your own interests but each of you to the interests of the others (Philippians 2:4).

SEVEN

Bilateral Mastectomy

It was a bittersweet moment as I prepared myself for my bilateral mastectomy. I couldn't wait to get the cancer out of my breast. Although the cancer was only in my right breast, I decided to have both of them removed. My decision was based on the possibility of recurrence, but I also didn't want one natural breast and one with an implant.

During my chemo infusions, I talked to other women who already had their surgery, and they gave me great advice. I told them I was searching the internet for things to buy to prepare me for surgery. I'm so thankful that because of their experiences, they knew exactly what I would need. And I'm so glad I didn't waste more money on things that I wouldn't use like I did before I shaved my head. They prepared me for what to expect after the surgery. I was told I would barely be able to move my arms and would need a lot of help. But the best advice I got was to buy button up shirts and pajamas since I wouldn't be able to lift my arms over my head.

Just as they had said, it was very difficult to move my arms. Even if I tried to move them, the pain wouldn't let me.

I couldn't even pick up a full cup of water, so my husband only filled it half way. Every day I got a little better, but the healing process was longer than what I expected.

One of the ladies that I talked to had her mastectomy before her chemotherapy. Because every treatment is different, I had to get my cancer under control before I could get my surgery done. The next week, after our first conversation, she brought me a belt that she had made. It had large pockets attached to it for the drains to fit into. How kind and thoughtful of her. That belt was so helpful, and I wore it day and night.

I'd never had a major surgery before, and I was a little worried that I might not wake up. It was a long surgery so I had to be put under anesthesia and that concerned me. I prayed a lot and asked others to pray as well. I told myself to stop worrying about it because I had to have the surgery regardless, so I put it in God's hand, just like I had done with everything else. By the time my surgery day arrived, I was at peace. I did learn anesthesia is a funny thing. One second I was talking and the next second (which seemed like a second but really was several hours), I was awake.

During my doctor's visit with the surgeon who was going to do the mastectomy, she asked me how attached I was to my nipples. I laughed and told her that I already decided that I didn't want to keep them. I felt since my breast was full of cancer and they were a part of my breasts, I didn't want them. She said, "Good, because you can't keep them anyway." I didn't ask her why because I didn't care.

I'm sure it's hard for some to understand the way I dealt with the cancer decisions I made, but it was a lot easier for me. Today I don't dwell on or think about any part of my cancer because I didn't know much about it in the first place.

My surgeon also mentioned she would test a couple of

my lymph nodes for cancer during the surgery. The results came back positive, so she removed multiple lymph nodes. Following my surgery, I had lymphedema in my right arm. I had to retrain myself to use my arm differently. Now I need to be careful not to cut or burn myself while I cook, which isn't easy. My arm hurts a little, all the time, but especially when I overuse it. But it's nothing that I can't handle. I wear a sleeve on my arm when I need to ease the pain and when I do things that I'm not supposed to. Lifting more than five pounds is not recommended, but I do it occasionally and then I pay for it later. I treat it as normally as possible. I know my lymphedema could have been much worse, and I'm so thankful that it doesn't swell that much. God is so good all the time!

I was a little sad to say goodbye to my breasts. I didn't cry, but I talked to them and told them that I was going to miss them and was sorry that this happened to them. And I told them that they would still be a part of me, but in a different way, with implants. I didn't feel I needed to take a picture. Saying goodbye was enough closure for me.

There were two parts to my surgery that required two different surgeons. The first surgeon did the bilateral mastectomy. Once it was completed, the plastic surgeon took over and did the reconstruction and put in the expanders.

When I woke up from my surgery, I was in a lot of pain. I had five drains attached to me, and my breasts were tightly wrapped. I had to keep them wrapped for a few days until my follow-up appointment. I was very uncomfortable, and my breasts were swollen and extremely sore. I constantly prayed and told myself *I'll be better tomorrow.* It was extremely painful to lay flat on my back so I slept on the recliner in my living room for almost three weeks. I took pain meds for about four days, and then I stopped. I was still in a lot of pain, but I didn't like the feeling of being tired all of the time.

It was a brutal surgery to get through, and my husband took two weeks off work to help me, which I needed and appreciated. He helped me do everything, and he constantly checked up on me because I couldn't even get myself up off the recliner. He took such great care of me throughout my entire journey. He had no problem helping me take a shower and get dressed. He also kept track of the fluid from my drains. Once the fluid got to the required level, I was able to get them removed. The most exciting part of my day was watching my fluid levels decrease.

We both felt it would be better if he kept track of my medications since I was pretty much out of it for a couple of days. I had to take an antibiotic and a pain medicine. I needed to take the antibiotic in the morning and at night and the pain medication every four to six hours. I took the pain medication every three hours when I felt the pain increasing. The day after my surgery was when I felt the most excruciating pain. I felt like I couldn't handle it. I told him that the pain medicine wasn't working. You should have seen the look on his face when he read the label. He realized he had mixed up the prescriptions. He was giving me the antibiotics instead of my pain medicine. He felt so bad, and I was so upset. I quickly forgave him because I love him. This is a part of my journey we laugh about today.

During the mastectomy, the plastic surgeon put expanders into my chest to stretch out my skin, and I had them in my chest for about six months. My skin needed to be stretched out as much as possible before they could place the implants.

I went to the surgeon's office every couple of weeks so he could slowly fill the expanders. It was a slow process to make sure my skin wouldn't die. It was very uncomfortable process, and the expanders hurt all the time. They hurt the most when I would lay down, and the worst part of all was that I had to learn to sleep on my back.

I have always had large breasts so I decided to down size tremendously. I used to be a size D cup. I figured I'm getting older and I don't need the backache or the shoulder pain from the bra straps. I had a hard time deciding on my new breast size so I asked my husband for his opinion. He told me the same thing multiple times. He said "It's your body; it's up to you." So, I made the decision to go a lot smaller.

After a mastectomy, there is no determining a cup size, but I'm guessing I'm about a small C cup. The one good thing about the expanders was that I was able to see how big or small I wanted to be before replacing them with the implants. The implants are a lot more comfortable than the expanders, but they are still a little painful at times. And since there isn't much fat in my breasts anymore, sometimes I can see the ripple of the implant through my skin, but it doesn't bother me.

I couldn't wait any longer to feel like myself again so about two and a half weeks after my surgery, I sat in my car thinking I could drive. As I started to back the car out of the driveway, I realized I couldn't do it. I was very determined to get myself back to normal as soon as possible so I tried again a few days later and this time I drove. I couldn't believe how sore my chest felt afterwards. I never realized how much we use our chest muscles to drive.

Soon after, I went to my surgeon for a follow up appointment. No, I didn't tell him I had been driving, but I did learn there is one advantage to having a mastectomy—I don't have to do a mammogram ever again! My breasts will never be smashed again. Now that's a relief and a happy thought.

Do not be anxious about anything, but in every situation, by prayer and petition, with thanksgiving, present your requests to God (Philippians 4:6).

EIGHT

My Healing!

There's no better way to describe God than to say, "He's not of this world." Those words are the absolute truth! Because of this revelation, I've struggled to convey exactly how I felt when He literally touched me, entered into my body, and healed me.

I've also learned that unless you go through it yourself, you truly can't understand. The closest comparison I can think of is what it feels like to become a parent. Before I had a child, I couldn't comprehend unconditional love. After having my first child, I understood what a powerful love it is and a love that I don't want to live without. I can't live without.

There are hundreds of thousands of words in our English language, but no words descriptive enough because His words aren't our words, and they don't have the same meaning as ours. I have spent months searching, struggling, praying, and crying out to God for the right words to share with the world. I probably always will because I want everyone to know what we are going to feel in heaven. I have relented to the fact that what I have experienced is near impossible to describe. I've searched the internet for synonyms, but I've found nothing because again, there are no words to explain what God has done for me.

Our words such as peace and joy can't be compared to His peace and His joy because His words emit completely different feelings—feelings our human bodies can't produce by themselves. The one and only word that I found that is even remotely close to describing the glory of God is supernatural. He is a supernatural God who is far beyond any of our thoughts and feelings and reaches far beyond anything that we have ever experienced. He is so surreal and beyond our imagination.

On the evening of December 16, 2017, I took a small piece of a muscle relaxer for the back pain I was experiencing. When I woke up the next morning, which was a Sunday, I felt a little tired and didn't really feel like going to church. I got out of bed to get ready but decided to lay back down for a while. One of the reasons for not wanting to go, other than being tired, was that in the afternoon I had plans. I figured if I did go to church, I would leave early during closing worship.

I usually meet my girlfriends at church, and we all sit together in the same place. They didn't show up that Sunday except for my friend who sings on the worship team. So I chose to sit in a completely different area that had the only two seated pew in the whole building. I sat next to a lady that I didn't even know, which was totally out of my comfort zone.

My church's routine is to worship before and after the pastor's message, but this Sunday, of all Sundays, it was different. After worship, before the message, everyone that led worship sat down on the stage and stayed up there the entire service, including my friend. I thought maybe there was going to be a special service because I have never seen them do that before. So this particular Sunday I sat alone the entire time. I truly believe it was all part of God's plan because He was going to heal me.

When the message was over, the worship team stood back up on stage and started to lead worship again. Instead of leaving as I had planned, I decided to stay for a song because it's my favorite part of church. I love to worship because worshiping through song always lifts my spirits.

It's such a beautiful thought, knowing my friend was singing while I was being healed. Knowing now that God controlled every step of my morning is completely amazing. God got me out of bed and made sure I sat alone at church so there wouldn't be any distractions. He was going to heal me! Wow! Doesn't that blow your mind!?

As closing worship began, I stood up and started to sing. A few moments later, as I was worshiping, I felt a gentle presence come over the lower left side of my leg. In the past I had experienced God's presence as a light breeze that would pass by or go through me. This was drastically different. It was a physical touch on the outside of my leg, and it continued to move very, very slowly up my side like the feeling when you slowly walk into a body of water and the water rises against your body as you go deeper and deeper.

For a couple of seconds, I couldn't figure out what I was feeling. I said to myself in a concerned voice, *What is that?* I was confused! As this feeling continued to move very slowly up my side and neared my hip, I gasped in shock and asked,

Oh…God is that you? Within a split second, He answered me by wrapping Himself around my entire body from head to toe. He surprised me because I didn't really expect Him to answer me.

As I was standing there physically covered in God's presence, I noticed my mood didn't change. I still felt tired and couldn't believe what I was feeling. I took a quick, deep breath, and said again, in a surprised voice, *Oh God it is you?* As soon as I acknowledged Him, He slowly went from the outside of my body to the inside.

His touch and presence that was completely wrapped around my body entered my body all at once. I was completely enveloped. From every angle of my body, He gradually started to move inward and met in the center of my body. It was beyond any feeling I have ever felt. The best way to describe how it felt as He entered into my body is, if you cross your arms and run your fingertips tenderly and gently down your arms until they meet.

Once He entered my body, it took me a second to realize He was healing me. I said again in great surprise, *Oh my gosh, You are healing me!* (Yes, I said "Oh my gosh" to God. I can't believe I said that but I did.) I thanked Him and told Him that I accepted His healing and that I truly loved Him.

As soon as I said that, my entire being changed! All at once everything became absolutely, miraculously beautiful. My body didn't feel the same. I instantly felt light as a feather, which made me feel like I was floating. My mind was different, and I wasn't able to think the way I had in my human body. The Holy Spirit had taken over my body and mind, and I was radiating in His peace, His glory, and His love.

He spoke to me and said, "Remember how you feel." I acknowledged Him and said, "Okay, I'll remember how I feel." It is very clear to me and I know that it was God talking to me and telling me to remember.

He spoke to me again and told me to start from my head and move to my feet. Then I acknowledged Him again and said, "Okay I'll start with my head." I focused on my mind, and it was completely clear—no worries and no anxious thoughts. I wasn't able to think of anything at all except how extremely happy and unbelievably peaceful I felt.

When I was worshiping, my eyes were open but during the actual healing, I believe God closed my eyes. I didn't see the darkness that we see when we close our eyes. I saw a soft yellowish color along with a very beautiful, subtle white. They weren't the same as our colors, and it's hard for me to explain because they were colors I'd never seen before. They were His colors and just like the Holy Spirit presented Himself to me in gentleness and softness, so did the colors. They almost seemed translucent, but I'm not sure if they actually were. It was so unbelievably beautiful! Feeling His love and seeing these magnificent colors made me feel like I was physically glowing. It was completely surreal and absolutely miraculous. He is beyond beautiful!

I felt His peace, joy, and glory all at once. They weren't separate emotions as we experience in our human minds. It was His astounding and powerful love. He is breathtaking! Saying He is beyond beautiful and provides extreme joy is an understatement. He is inconceivable. Feeling the feelings only He can give all at once created a supernatural form of peace and happiness in me.

I was at complete peace, but it's a peace that is incomprehensible to our finite mind. And I felt a happiness so deep within that when I think about it today, I can barely handle it. The happiness that He gave me created an overwhelming sense of joy. It's a happiness I don't want to continue to live my life without, but knowing one day it's going to be for eternity is unfathomable. Think of life's happiest moment and multiply it by infinity and repeat it infinitely more times and never stop. And it still won't compare to the happiness only He can give.

I know I was standing, or was I? I felt weightless and I had to really concentrate on my feet because I could barely feel the floor underneath me. Since I didn't feel one ounce of my body weight or the pressure from standing, it took me a second to realize that I was actually still standing. Also, I didn't hear any noise around me. It was peacefully quiet. I didn't hear the worship music playing until I started concentrating on what I was hearing. It was very faint and sounded a mile away.

I was still me, but a different me. He didn't take away the core of me. I felt like me. I knew that the feelings I was having were from Him. My human thoughts were completely gone. My body and mind were different. I was filled with His spirit, which is why I didn't feel my body and mind. It was absolutely a supernatural God flowing in and through me. It was a supernatural experience because He is a supernatural God!

Once I remembered what I was feeling from head to toe, He slowly started to leave my body. He began to drape Himself off of me like a blanket, but I like to think of it being His robe sliding off of me. It was as if the blanket was sliding off of me and dropping to the floor but very, very slowly, which gave me time to beg. I felt Him leave but only on my right side. It took me awhile after my healing to realize that He left on my right side to take my cancer with Him. Praise God!

As He began to leave, I begged him, "Please don't go! No, no, no don't go! No, God please don't go!" I begged like I never begged before because I didn't want the experience to end. I could have stood there for the rest of my life.

Then I noticed the music starting to get louder. It was like turning up the volume on the radio but very gradually. The music was loud again, and my body and mind were back to normal, my new normal.

Those beautiful colors that I was experiencing were gone, and the darkness in my closed eyes was back. I kept my eyes closed because I was afraid to open them. I seriously felt like I was glowing but wasn't sure if I was. I don't like attention drawn to me, and I was afraid everyone was staring at me. I prayed and asked God not to let everyone be staring at me. So, I squinted my eyes and peeked to see what was happening around me, and thank God everyone was still worshiping.

I looked at the lady standing next to me to see if she noticed anything, but it was obvious she hadn't. Looking back, I wish I would have asked her what I was doing or how I was standing during my healing.

I stood in complete disbelief at what just happened. I don't know how long my healing took because it felt as if time stood still.

After it was over, I didn't know which way to turn, and I felt myself starting to panic. I wanted to run up on stage and tell everyone what had just happened, but I stopped myself.

Then I thought I should go tell the pastor who was worshiping in the front row, but I didn't. My mind was scrambling, and I needed to calm myself down so I decided to leave before worship was over as I had planned. It was the most exciting and happiest moment of my life. Thank You, God, for my beautiful healing!

When I got into my car, I sat there for a couple of minutes because I was trying to process what I had just experienced. I kept asking myself, "What just happened?" I knew I was healed, but I couldn't believe what a beautiful and powerful experience I just went through.

As I was driving home, that familiar spinning in my mind began. I was wondering how I was going to tell everyone and who would actually believe what just happened. When I got home, I told my family that I was healed at church. I shared the story, and my husband looked at me and nodded his head. My boys were happy but didn't have much of a response, even though I knew they believed me.

I know I had an out of body experience. God lifted me out of my body to experience His glory and to let everyone know how unbelievably happy and at peace we are going to be in heaven. I can't conceive the thought of standing in heaven looking around with God by my side. I can't wait to meet Him and give Him a big hug, but I will probably fall to my knees first. And I can't wait to hear His voice and talk to Him. It overwhelms me with extreme excitement. Heaven is beyond our imagination, and we are going to have "awe moments" for eternity, and I simply can't wait!

I would do anything to be touched by God again. I would battle breast cancer over and over again for the rest of my life, without a doubt, if I were guaranteed He would come back to me every time.

How extremely beautiful and amazing that I was healed and hugged by God. I know I was healed to let the world know that He is real.

Lord my God, I called to you for help, and you healed me (Psalms 30:2).

NINE

Radiation

Three days after my healing, I was scheduled to do a CT scan before I started my radiation treatments. There was a constant struggle within me, not knowing whether I should continue with my treatment or if I should walk away from it, after God healed me.

It was frustrating because I knew deep down that I was supposed to walk away, but I was afraid of what people would think of my decision. Yes, I'm strong and don't usually care about what others think, but this was different. I worried about what my family and friends would think or say to me about how I could possibly stop my treatment especially with such an aggressive cancer. I knew it would be hard for them to understand but especially hard for those who didn't have a relationship with God.

I decided to finish what I started, and I began my radiation treatments. While I was in the CT scanner, I knew I was wasting my time. I asked God to forgive me, and I told Him that I was sorry. I felt a guilt that I had to put in the back of my head because I felt ashamed. I'm so thankful He forgives.

I had no doubt in my mind that the CT scan was not going to show any sign of cancer. I knew the results would come back negative, and they did. Praise God!

At my next appointment, even though I knew the answer, I asked the doctor if she saw any cancer in my CT scan. She said no. No surprise there! She said, "If it was there, I would see it." I sat there thanking God over and over. I couldn't stop thanking Him.

During every radiation treatment, I just knew I was radiating my breast for no reason. Every time I laid on the table and looked straight up at the radiation machine, I said, "I'm sorry, God." I know telling Him once is enough, but I felt this was different and I needed to tell Him every time.

A few days prior, He had physically entered my body and healed me, and now I had a machine above me radiating nothing. I was disappointed in myself. Again, I put this guilt in the back of my mind because it was too painful to think about how afraid I was to talk about what God had done for me. I know God understood my decision making as I relied on Him in making these decisions.

I prayed for my skin not to get too burned from the radiation. My skin got red, like a mild sunburn, but I am thankful because I know it could have been a lot worse. I put a pain relief cream on the areas that felt tender, and as soon as my treatment was over, it went away fairly quickly.

My right breast became firm from the radiation. It will always stay firm no matter how old I get, and it will never sag. I kind of wish they could have radiated my left breast too so they would match, but of course that didn't happen. Now I have a firm radiated breast and a normal one. Eventually, the normal one will drop with time and age. They say no two breasts are alike anyway. Thank God for plastic surgeons.

About a month after I started my radiation treatments, my radiologist told me that I didn't need the last week of my treatment. I couldn't believe it! I knew right then and there that God put a stop to it. I knew the doctor's decision was based on God's timing. He protected me even when I made the decision to start the radiation treatments. He is nothing but love! The doctor said, "You don't look too happy about it." I guess the expression on my face didn't convey what my heart was feeling. I told her, "You have no idea," and I chuckled under my breath. I covered my face with my hands and thanked God.

One of my biggest regrets is that I didn't share my healing with my radiologist. I wanted to so badly! At every appointment as we talked, I said to myself, *Tell her,* but I never did. I know I should have but I wasn't quite ready.

Shortly after my radiation ended, I had an appointment with my oncologist. I told her that the radiologist cut my treatment short. She wasn't too happy about it, and she didn't seem to understand why.

I shared my healing with her, not knowing if she had a personal relationship with God. I am still not sure if she is a believer, but she respected my story. I was so nervous sharing with her because it was out of my comfort zone. I had only shared with my family and friends, and that was much easier. This was my first time sharing with someone, not knowing where they stood spiritually, and it was the best feeling.

As soon as we were finished talking, she turned to the computer and started talking about Letrozole. It's a daily pill that cancer survivors take for years that helps prevent cancer from returning. I thought to myself, *Why is she talking about this pill when I just told her I was healed?* but I understood because it was her responsibility as my doctor to inform me about it. She was adamant that I take the pill. She actually had me thinking about it.

The struggle was and is real. So, I decided to take the pill. I was taking it daily and then I thought, *Why am I taking a pill that I don't need?* I continued to struggle with my decision. So, I started to take it every couple of days, but as soon I would take the pill, it felt wrong, and I felt guilty. I cut it down to a few times a week. To be honest, I still take it a few times a week, but I'm hoping I will eventually stop.

After my healing, I went to get my routine blood work done, and the results came back normal. She said she was very pleased. At my follow up visit she actually said they were excellent!

You are my refuge and my shield; I have put my hope in your word (Psalm 119:114).

.

TEN

Hysterectomy

My entire journey originally began with a trip to the ob-gyn for unresolved pain in my abdomen. The ob-gyn found severe endometriosis and recommended I have a hysterectomy right away. A couple of months after I completed my radiation treatment, it was finally time for my hysterectomy. I had a total hysterectomy with bilateral salpingo-oophorectomy, which is the removal of the uterus, cervix, fallopian tubes, and ovaries. I was originally scheduled to have my hysterectomy the same day I started my first chemotherapy treatment. Isn't that ironic? Once I was diagnosed with cancer, my hysterectomy was put on hold until my treatment was over.

In the meantime, my oncologist gave me a Lupron shot every month to take away the pain and bleeding that I was experiencing. I was so excited to get my last Lupron shot. It felt like a little milestone because it was one less trip I had to make to that doctor, and it was one step closer to the end of my journey with cancer.

I had multiple cysts in my ovaries, and it was most

painful when one burst. Thank God it only happened once. The doctor mentioned that during surgery they were going to test my ovaries for cancer. I prayed and trusted God that the results would come back negative, and of course, they did.

I asked God for an easy recovery. I felt it would be, considering everything I had already been through. The only disappointment about my hysterectomy is that I had to stay in the hospital overnight. I tried leaving right after the surgery, but they wouldn't let me. I absolutely hate staying in hospitals, and yes, hate is a strong word.

Since I couldn't leave, I asked my husband to hand me my cell phone so I could check my emails and start working. I felt fine! I was a little groggy from the anesthesia, but that didn't stop me. I made phone calls five minutes after I woke up from surgery. As I was reading an email the words were a little blurry and I thought to myself, *Who does this?* Me. I do!

When the doctor walked into my hospital room, he talked about the surgery. He said that he almost had to cut me open because my endometriosis was so much worse than he expected. I thanked him for not giving up, and then I couldn't stop thanking God. That probably would have been a much more difficult recovery.

Other than walking a little slower than normal for a few days, the recovery was really quite easy for me and was no comparison to my previous surgeries. I was up and around right away, and of course, I was driving a couple days afterward, even though I wasn't supposed to.

I had a follow-up appointment scheduled about a week after my surgery, and I told my doctor that I had been driving for days. He laughed and said that cancer survivors are his favorite patients. I said, "That's right because we can do anything." He agreed.

The only reason I had been dreading a hysterectomy was because I thought my mood swings and hot flashes would get a lot worse. That's the rumor I had heard. I had already been going through menopause and experiencing them for over three years. My mood swings had never been that bad, but my hot flashes were a whole different story.

Throughout the years of talking to other woman about hysterectomies, I heard that once a woman has a total hysterectomy her hormones get out of whack, and her moods and hot flashes can get unbearable. Remembering these stories made me not want to do the surgery, but once again I knew I had to. So I prayed as I always did. I figured nowadays there are different ways to keep those symptoms under control so I thought it wouldn't be a big deal. As much as I talk to my body and with God's strength, I knew I would be fine.

After the surgery I waited day after day to feel a difference in my body, but I never did. After a few months passed, I realized the surgery hadn't changed my body or my mind. Thank God! I was literally anticipating a change in my mood, but it never happened. I was also waiting for my hot flashes to increase, which I didn't think was possible, but they didn't. Nothing changed. Everything is the same as it was before the surgery. Thanks to God. He continues to amaze me.

Hysterectomies do change some women, but it didn't change me. Everybody is different, so another lesson learned. Once again I learned just because something happens to someone else doesn't mean it's going to happen to me. The learning never ends.

If I had to choose my favorite surgery, it would be this one. Not only because it was a breeze to recover from, but I don't have monthly periods anymore. Now that's a reason to celebrate, right, ladies?

Before I was diagnosed with cancer, I used to buy over-the-counter products to control my mood and hot flashes. My oncologist suggested that I try a plant based and hormone free pill which does keep my mood normal but doesn't completely take away my hot flashes.

Recently I have been hearing about health benefits from taking turmeric. I decided to buy it in pill form, and after taking it for about a month, I noticed I was hardly having any hot flashes. I couldn't believe it, but it took away fifty percent of my hot flashes. I know our bodies are different, and it may or may not work for everyone, but I am hoping the information and knowledge I have gained will ultimately help at least one person.

The Lord himself goes before you and will be with you; he will never leave you nor forsake you. Do not be afraid; do not be discouraged (Deuteronomy 31:8).

Eleven

Reconstruction Surgery

As this seemingly impossible journey neared the end, I was so excited to have my first reconstructive surgery. At this point I'd already had two surgeries so I wasn't nervous at all. I was thrilled to get those awful expanders exchanged for implants. This recovery was painful, but it was much easier than the bilateral mastectomy.

I anxiously waited for the day to come. In fact, I was so excited that the last few days I started to count down the days. I couldn't wait to see how my breasts were going to look. Throughout my life I had never even thought about getting breast implants, but here I was getting them after all.

My new breast size wasn't a concern to me. I knew they were going to end up much smaller than before, and they are. I figured no matter what size they were going to be, I'd be happy with them, and I am. It was a good decision to downsize.

Before the surgery, I had a choice to reconstruct my breasts with implants or to take fatty tissue from a different part of my body and put it into my breasts. For some strange reason, my mind was very set on getting implants. I didn't think twice about my options, and I felt it would be weird to put fat from a different part of my body into my breasts. I really don't know why I thought that way because breasts are fat. My mind was so set on the implants that I didn't even research the benefits or drawbacks. Today, I feel that was a big mistake. I wish I would have researched the pros and cons of each procedure before I made such a big decision. I didn't realize that the implants would be so uncomfortable. Another lesson learned.

My reconstructive surgery day had finally arrived, and I was so thrilled. My husband took me and stayed in the waiting room throughout the entire surgery to make sure I was doing well. When I woke up from surgery, I had one drain attached to each of my sides near my breasts, which was so much easier than the five from the mastectomy.

I had a bit of a hard time waking up from the surgery. I recall very little, but I do remember telling the nurse I was in a lot of pain and that I needed more medicine so she gave me a shot. But before she did, she startled me because I wasn't completely awake, and I woke up to her literally shoving a cracker in my mouth. What I really meant to say was that I was feeling nauseous. So as you can imagine, it was not a fun car ride home. My poor husband. When we got home, he continued to take great care of me. This time he didn't mix up my medications, thank God.

A few days later, I got the drains removed, and I really felt like this surgery wasn't such a big deal. I was cooking and doing some light cleaning around the house shortly after. Even though I promised my surgeon that I wouldn't do these things, I did them anyway. He told me prior to the surgery that this one would feel like night and day from my bilateral mastectomy. He was right, but he had no idea whom he was talking to—his strongest patient. I was able to move my arms, and I only took pain meds for a couple of days.

About five months later, I had my second reconstructive surgery, but when the time came, I was so over it. I'm so grateful for my healing and for all the great doctors God put in my path, but by this time I had been through so much, there wasn't anything I couldn't handle. I already had five months of chemo, a bilateral mastectomy, radiation, a total hysterectomy, and one reconstructive surgery, all within a year and a half. And not to mention all of the doctor's appointments in between. I kept myself mentally and physically strong by continuing to talk to myself and by drawing near to God.

I thought I knew exactly what to expect for my second reconstructive surgery so I didn't think it was going to be a big deal. I had a lot of scar tissue built up on my side near my right breast from the previous reconstructive surgery. My right arm didn't lay flat against my body so my surgeon suggested doing liposuction during the surgery to flatten it out. Again, maybe I should have researched the pros and cons of liposuction. Or one would think that I should have learned by then to start asking questions. The procedure ended up being very painful for over six months, and it still bothers me today when I lay on my right side. It looks great, but I will never do any type of liposuction ever again.

To this day, I still need to have more surgeries, and I understand reconstructive surgery is a process, but it's a process that I'm not willing to risk right now. To be honest, I'm not sure if I will have any more. If I do decide to have another surgery, it will definitely be my last one. I have no idea how people have repeat plastic surgeries.

After my second reconstructive surgery, I didn't see much of a change in my breasts so I was a little disappointed. The little change I did see was a slight difference in the shape of my breasts, and my cleavage was even and that looked really good. I was hoping the scars that were showing from the first surgery would have been tucked away, but they had gotten a little worse. Even though I am not completely satisfied with the way they look, I can live with it. After all that I've been through, I have learned they are just breasts.

When I was at my doctor's appointment to get my drains out, I had a really bad anxiety attack. This was the only anxiety attack I had throughout my battle. I used to have anxiety attacks when I was younger, and the last one I had was about five years before my diagnosis.

The anxiety attack was triggered by the nurse when she started to pull out the drain from my side. The drain was stuck because it was wrapped around my implant. The reason I knew it was wrapped around my implant is because when she finally got it out, I felt it unravel around my breast. It was the weirdest feeling. It took all of her body weight to pull it out. She was leaning her body against mine for support to pull as hard as she possibly could. I kept telling myself that it was almost over and praying to God to help me get through it. Actually, I was begging Him. I even noticed her arms were slightly shaking because she was using all of her strength to pull. I mentally couldn't take it anymore. It was enough to send me into a panic. Usually when I feel an attack coming on, I can talk myself out of it, but this time there was no way. I tried my best to control it, but it was way too much for me to handle.

While the nurse was pulling as hard as possible, the doctor walked into the room. He sat down and started to talk to me about my next surgery. I was dumbfounded. I couldn't believe he was talking to me as if he didn't see anything that was happening. I was overwhelmed. That was the final straw, and my anxiety attack began. I couldn't breathe, my chest was pounding, and I started to sweat really bad. I didn't hear a word the doctor said. The doctor noticed I was having a hard time as I'm sure my facial expression was a dead give away, so he said we should continue the conversation later. To this day, I haven't gone back.

Once she got the drain out, I wanted to get up and leave but the nurse wouldn't let me. She told me that I didn't look very good, but I told her I was fine. I looked in the mirror and my face was sweaty and pale. She needed to make sure I was okay before she released me. She gave me a bottle of water and took my blood pressure, but it was high so I had to wait for it to go down. It was a hard appointment to get through. I couldn't wait to leave because I knew I physically and mentally needed a long break. That was a very memorable last day of my journey.

For a while I considered nipple tattooing. Most of the area on my breasts is numb from the surgeries so I figured it wouldn't be painful. It's amazing nowadays how the tattoo artists do 3D nipple tattooing. They make them look so real. When I discussed the tattooing with my husband, he made a valid point, which changed my mind. He asked, "Will the tattoo drop or become misshaped when your breast drops as you get older?" I laughed because it was a funny visual. I told him, "I don't know but it makes sense." Since my left breast will drop in time, I feel the tattoo might become misshapen too. I know that is something I don't want to happen because it would really bother me.

After we joked about it, we had a serious conversation. He told me it was up to me, and it doesn't bother him the way they look. Since it doesn't bother either of us, I decided not to tattoo them. I also felt it would be weird to see nipples but not be able to feel them. It seemed to trigger the same feelings I had thinking about watching my hair fall out. I actually like the way my breasts look without nipples. I know a lot of women who were excited to get their breasts tattooed, and I'm happy for them, but it's not for me. If I were younger, I would have definitely tattooed something on my breasts, like flowers.

Cast all your anxiety on him because he cares for you (1 Peter 5:7).

TWELVE

My Journey Begins

What I want you to know is that God will meet you right where you are. He did me! He met me exactly where I was. I don't read my Bible every day. I don't go to weekly Bible studies. I don't even go to church every Sunday. But God still met me. He took the Anna He created in His image, and He met me right where I was: in my brokenness, in my vulnerability, in my weakness. Isaiah 57:18a says, "I have seen their ways, but I will heal them." He chose to heal me because I had faith. I had faith and confidence in the God I knew. I acknowledged Him and He answered. He says in Matthew 17:20,

> *Because you have so little faith. Truly I tell you, if you have faith as small as a mustard seed, you can say to this mountain, "Move from here to there," and it will move. Nothing will be impossible for you.*

I am here to tell you that you don't have to have it all together for God to meet you where you are. He uses any and all of us who call on His name for His purpose. Psalm 57:2

says ,"I cry out to God Most High, to God, who vindicates (delivers) me."

Immediately after my healing, I had to share with my friend who was up on stage singing on the worship team. She's the friend who was raised in the church (a pastor's kid), who was at church at least two times a week, attended weekly Bible studies, and was went to church summer camps, winter camps, and mission trips. If anyone should believe me, it would be her. I asked her if she believed me, and she said, "Yes, I believe you because everything you've told me is supported through scripture in the Bible." I didn't know that. I said, "Really!" God knew exactly who I was supposed to share with. Amazing!

From that moment on, she shared scripture after scripture supporting my story. I couldn't believe what I was reading. Especially the verse John 14:27, which reads,

Peace I leave with you; my peace I give you. I do not give to you as the world gives. Do not let your hearts be troubled and do not be afraid.

After I read that verse, I started bawling. I knew that verse was directed specifically toward me because it was exactly what I experienced. Tears of joy come to my eyes every time I read it.

Before my diagnosis, I stressed about things. If I only knew then what I know now, I would've lived a different life. I've always appreciated everything and everyone in my life, but now I appreciate every day more than I did before. I have learned to let go of the small stuff and to stop worrying about things I have no control over. It took most of my life to realize that stress doesn't change the outcome. I used to wake up and go to bed stressed about anything and everything.

This trial has taught me what is important and what's not. In my opinion, one of the most important things in this life is good health. Just knowing my family and friends are healthy brings me so much comfort. Since I don't sweat the small stuff anymore, my life is much more peaceful. Most of all, my journey changed my relationship with God. I couldn't live one second of the day without Him.

After my healing, you would think I would be floating on cloud nine, but I wasn't. I knew it was a blessing but wrapped in that blessing was a huge struggle. I've struggled for months wondering, *Why me? Why did He choose to heal me and not my girlfriend who died from breast cancer? Why me and not so many others?* I've cried many nights, not knowing why He chose me.

As I mentioned before, I know that I was healed to let the world know that God is real and He heals, but I still found myself searching for an answer other than He loves me. I do know that He knows. He knows why He chose to heal me. One day I will have my answer when I'm called home, and that is satisfying. He is a faithful God, and He indeed answers prayers.

We are all God's children and He shows favor on all of us in different ways. Maybe sometimes we don't always realize it, but I know every good thing in my life is from Him. I thank Him every day for His favor on me and my healing. I am forever grateful.

I've been learning to listen more intently, to simply be quiet and hear Him speak. When I listen, I'm much wiser in discerning what is from Him. I'm learning to obey God every time He speaks to me.

I believe everyone has a purpose. I thought there was no greater purpose than being a mom. Being a mom is the most fulfilling part of my life. My greatest joy! I know my boys are gifts from God, and I thank Him for them every day.

During this trial, God showed me His purpose and plan for my life. It is crystal clear to me the direction He wants me to follow. I believe I had to battle for my life to find my true purpose, which is honoring Him in everything; the good, the bad, and the horrible. I will spend the rest of my life honoring Him in all that I do, and I will speak about Him to anyone who will listen.

I feel like I'm just beginning to live my life at fifty. This is the beginning of my new life. It's a life that is completely in God's hands. I am excited to share my God experience with the world for the rest of my life. I strongly feel that God didn't take me home because it wasn't my time. He still has work to do through me. It brings me great joy that God has faith in me to achieve His purpose for my life.

A few months after my healing, God put this book on my heart. It was a prompting that got stronger and stronger every day. I trust my God experience will give you strength and help you on your journey to completely trust Him in everything. He is real, and sometimes He isn't what you expect Him to be. He is much, much more, and He is beyond beautiful. He is God.

Trust in the Lord with all your heart and lean not on your own understanding; in all your ways submit to him, and he will make your paths straight (Proverbs 3:5-6).

Connect with Anna

Anna's greatest desire is that her message provides hope and brings comfort to others. She wrote her story, believing that it would help you or someone you know get through some of the seemingly darkest days of life.

Anna is active on social media and would love to hear about your journey. She knows the importance of a strong community and wants to build that with her readers. Please contact her for guidance, support, or with any concerns you may have. Her mission in life is to help others, which, in turn, brings her great joy!

Contact Information
Website: itwasnotmytime.com
Facebook: It Was Not My Time
Instagram: itwasnotmytime
Twitter: itwasnotmytime